Unfounded

Michael Trocchia

FUTURECYCLE PRESS
www.futurecycle.org

Library of Congress Control Number: 2014959375

Copyright © 2015 Michael Trocchia
All Rights Reserved

Published by FutureCycle Press
Lexington, Kentucky, USA

ISBN 978-1-938853-60-9

for Alison

Contents

FATALISMS

Homecoming..9
Of Shelter and Form...10
Undo Forces..12
Inscription for a Chorus..14
Determinism..16
Man Goes Out for Walk, Finds Dagger, Etc..................22
Not for us...24
Irreparably..25
Intersections..26

SUBSTANCE SAID

Gifts of Verse..31
Motion in a Path to Myself...32
The Metaphysician Goes Home..................................34
Poem Without Itself...36
Unsparing...37
I Am Architect..38
Erosion...40
Nonsense of Self..42
Poem Under a Paperweight.......................................43
Desire...44
Without Reference...46

GUESSWORKED

Verum and Factum...53
Studies of Rainwork...54
The Parts of Clay Birds..56
Playing House..58
An Invitation to Speak...60
Curse of the Self-sufficient.......................................62
The Idler Puts Himself at Risk..................................63
Guesswork...66
Acknowledgments

FATALISMS

Homecoming

When he returns, the house itself
is displaced, roots removed. Chairs
kicked over. The olive table split. A spilt
glass of dried wine. Unfamiliar footprints
across the tile floor. The proud walls
of the upper halls peeling with pictures
of some strange family. The un-
welcoming made sharp, set like knives
in a drawer thrust open, fallen off
track. Nothing turns toward him, not
the dust-covered blades of the fan, not
the heads of ragged dolls, not the rusted
knobs of cobwebbed cabinets, nor the ghost
of a woman he believed would stay.
The bedroom door is a wooden hand
pushing him in. The vanity stiff
with years. The mattress cover
tossed about like a map for exiles.
Before he can close his eyes, the house
itself falls asleep, shuts him in the eaves
of an uninhabitable dream.

Of Shelter and Form

We meet outside
to be misunderstood.
Someone points the way

to something made up,
to a fence built around
the others. But a school boy

leads us indoors. His father
turns on the air. We mime
a family of ourselves to stay

warm. This is all very new
in a house of frost. One
of us learns his name

is on the ceiling. One
of us buries his hands
in a dream of falling

temperatures. Someone
throws a stone outdoors.
The storm door knocks

us over. The floor is torn
with teeth and the shades
are blown thin. One

of us is having sex
in the basement. I discover
that I am asking how

death is possible in light
of all this. I am an average
man with nothing to hide

himself in. I am told to sit
down in a light that takes
things along. We are taken

out back to lose track
of ourselves. One of us hangs
on the last word of another.

Undo Forces

Hand it to yourself,
friend, the dust of this

faraway coinage. Find
yourself in the nth

country, under its ought—
bitten skies, be amused

by the shouts
of its shattering

boys in brass. Instigate
the landscape, its damning

effect. Come away
from it. All of us will

run from the nth
country. So be

good. Roam with us
who roam like geese

through widening streets
where a trumpet erupts

inside the skull,
into a troubling

form of hillside
and hollow.

Inscription for a Chorus

Put us inside
earth, for we are
the dying.
Touch our backs
to a fathoming
of crust, for we are

unminding, emptied
of moving
light, our gaze
absorbed in small
hours; for we are

heart-pressed
against indiscriminate
fate, no more
its faint idea. For us

a plot is made
hollow; no matter
the depth, so remnants
of this grave

voice might swell

well beyond the night
watchman's dream.

Determinism

The determinist is hard
at work. He is writing

a book—inside
will be found

a description
upon descriptions
of a going

always inside

out. This is how
    sentences, it will say,

        outrun themselves—
        for instance, a woman runs

        into now. What she passes
        places

        her in need
        of a thing

    greater than
    can be

    and she
    herself flees

    the moment
    she steps inside

    the maze
    of it.

The determinist's book will be
a hard one to close.

—

The determinist walks down
the street. The determinist
buys a paper. The determinist
looks at a woman.
An event like any
other begins to be

no event at all.
A woman is
in the house. A woman is

in the bedroom. A woman is
in the bed. A state of affairs
like any other

begins to be

another state
of affairs.

The face of it all
comes to a halt.

We blush
where it might have

kept going.

—

The determinist falls
asleep at his desk. He has been
thinking all day. He has been thinking
of the woman who will appear

in his book. It is late, much too late
to be at one's desk. Others have

gone home. The determinist is
by himself, at his desk, dreaming
of the woman who will appear

somewhere in his book.
He can dream this simply
because a woman once stood
still by his side, simply
because things run their course, simply
because his dreaming must be

otherwise.

The determinist
awakens to an alarming

thought—an unlikelihood,
sure, but now

that he is awake
it is certain

he must leave
things as they are

that instant.

—

There is one day, another
day, on which the determinist

is found dead. His death
is an ordinary affair, says

the woman who appears

inside his book. She continues
as if she were a thing running

off course:

>People enact
their accidents.
Emergency without

>what went wrong

>is the pool
of blood reflecting

>the course of events.
The sirens make sense

of noise. Things go
right and then

the chance
to die on time

is saved for later.

Much later she adds:

The threat of things
happening as they should.

The world accomplishes itself.
Its efficiency lets us
go—

the hum and must follow—

Her description
is that of a hard woman

to shut up inside
a book. A hard

woman to keep
close.

Man Goes Out for Walk, Finds Dagger, Etc.

After Oswald Spengler

I was out and about—
hampered by a shining
waistcoat. The night felt
uncut, a swollen instinct

inside the skin. I had the honor
of short breaths, the pity of earth,
pith of air. So I was faint, damned

to be inexact, fat and too far
along the footpath, or I was
not told otherwise. It happened
that people came to see me

lie down, be civil, hold out
one hand. Drink, they said
as I drank. I met each one
with my face. My eyes

gained a small advantage.
What they called

flavored I called fate,
vaguely. What they called
savory I called salvation, perhaps

a coin tossed high. Oh I had
the pleasure of honest looks,
seated children, around me:
a choice of weapons. Their hero

had failed them, fled, and so
soon after, as it would
have it, my name rang
with good cheer. A single year

wore away. I took one of them
as my wife. She sniveled. My arms
folded toward evening. The house
sighed like a fat man. I gathered

the sharpest words under
my breath. I pivoted, made
great strides, then bored

myself with a dagger
from an even darker age.

Not for us

Always a man fallen
deep in the wood—
a man not for us

to know. At dusk,
his wounds catch fire.

Irreparably

A fine death
lines the river-
man's throat

song, and down-
stream bend
heads of stunted

men, blind-
folded, some final
faltering judgment

not for them
to make. And in low-
lands, this hum of old

heat still, hell's white
noise burning the air
we grieve

into God's brow.

Intersections

He drags a rowboat of concepts
into a city. He is a boy at night
wearing the word *object*
on his hat. He thinks
the pledge of allegiance is
how to make love in the future.

A woman of possible names
is dressed in the outstretched
idea of youth. She sits in the boat
and holds too much in one hand,
a portion of herself in the other.

He breathes in the weight
of a man's heart and pulls
the boat off the street.
He has no reason to speak
but hears himself call her.

A building shadows his voice.
He kneels to see how the architecture
of this moment has confused them both.
A window opens, and when the time
comes his confessions will be glass.

She waits until he understands
the vanishing point of her eyes.
His reasons will begin with sense
and end with question marks.
She will do what can be done.

SUBSTANCE SAID

Gifts of Verse

I wanted to give you
the odor of ruined
gods, the double
fortune of summer's
end, the mild sorrow
borrowed from wounds
too small to hurt. I wanted
to give you the giver's
final breath, the taker's
right to take, the substance
of deadening verse.

Motion in a Path to Myself

I grip the sudden
memory and fade

against the insane
star. I stuff the shapeless

wind with some raw
idea of it and pause

before the opening
gate. I devise the flat

escape and then axe
the wrists of the witness

in me. My hands break
into birdsong under

breath. I yield the eye
and turn the ear inside

out for the whispering
sufficiency of things

near. My face grows
clockwise. It strikes me

each time I look back.

The Metaphysician Goes Home

for Leibniz's Law

I began life with a haircut,
new shoes. Call it an inclination
towards metaphysics. Bearing
certain new properties, I was not

myself all over again. Being
like a new man, I was

no longer certain
of whose shoes
I never had. Call it a break

not with anything particular,
just the form in which it comes.
Custom moods and the way
things turn in sunlight, an unalterable

place to turn in
myself, a kind

of coming home
to a house that's not mine.

Yes, new like someone
else's memory, I was

calling myself
in an empty room.

Poem Without Itself

You lift one side
of the poem. Each

word slides
        off
the page.
     Only punctuation
remains,
leaving this

    ordered silence—

a sheet of nothing
riddled
     with periods

of loss.

Unsparing

Your palm covers
this poem, pushes it
back into the page. Nothing

like the silence, you think,
of words that suffocate.

I Am Architect

I am architect, lean
and leaning. I name
the interior shadow
palpable, thin, uneasy.
In strain, layered in
double light, I am fugal
in the fault of lovers new
to consequence, embalmed
in idea of stone and weighed
embrace, blocked in
the pale field of cool
failures. Paved angular
around corner, I am
the alternate grammarian,
sad with tongue, slighted
under a sag of sun run
through the bent
sentence to some remote
build of question.
In the house of ten
thousand doors, I am
growing architecture
in a natural moment

of silence, for I am placed
there as even opening
and opening, way inside
the glass harm of our ways.

Erosion

Our boy of salt winds
eating ice by the sea

is thin as if to say this
syllable of nature

leaves bone
lost to water

and waiting. We sigh
wide silence of air

and allow him to while
away vowels of a long

sentence we thought
ourselves swallowing.

In time he will turn
mourner of stone

mouths. The dying will
let fall our calendar

mask. In the ruins
of his name our boy

must see himself
misspelt, unlettered

even, a child of form-
lessness and sands.

Nonsense of Self

Ears fall away silently.
Eyes drift out of focus.
Nose blown by foul winds.
Mouth stuffed with these words.
Hands tied to their final touch.

Poem Under a Paperweight

The sky is brought down
like a great weight.

Look at him: he is a kid
folding the sky into stone.

Look at him: he is a kid
crushing a great bird

under the word for it.

The sky is brought down
like too many shreds

of paper, brought down
like too many things

to repeat.

Look at him: he is a kid
without speech.

Look at him at the end
of a trembling

beneath us.

Desire

is your face
being drawn

away from the gray
draftsman. He works

because he is moved
to pass the time. He works

in a pale light
on the bridge

of your nose.
About to nod off,

his head jerks open.
How he darkens

the space just
beneath your gaze.

He can only guess
the way around

your tongue, how it lies
in a closed space.

And the proportions
of his eventual sleep

shape your skull
to paper. Your image

begins with him, here in
the way he looks

and looks—
disquietude in the ink

of your eyes is mis-
taken for dream.

He gives you his
jaw, a fat mouth, opens

your lips and with this
asks you a question

but your face
is somewhere else.

Without Reference

I took away names
of things, beginning

with the trees. *They
have each other,* I

barked, as I climbed
down the ladder, my

basket in hand, and
in it were *Cypress*

and *Fig, Muscle-
wood* and *Pine.*

Trees no longer
fixed to anything

but their dead
even sway. I took

the names of light
stone, bled them

one after the other
into an unending

creek—downstream
a doe drank consonants

mixed with minerals
and backwater. I took

the names of quiet
animals, hauled them

away in a man-sized
sack made from Latin

and burlap. I took
off with the names

of ancient gardens,
hid them within plain

sight of their petals
and shade. I snapped

the names off countries,
set fire to them, heard

history in the crackling
pronunciation. I peeled

off the names of fruit
and set them outside

a woman's mouth
to rot. I then took

names of our beloved
towers and scraped

the night skies
with their vowels.

And when you agreed
to take away names

of gods

they stole ours, used them
to little effect. Now we call

ourselves without
reference and small

acts of gods

have since been
committed in our name.

GUESSWORKED

Verum and Factum

After Giambattista Vico

What to be made
of sparrows stuck

in the throat? What
to be made of the girl

gasping in the shed,
of dead trees holding up

sheaves of white sky,
of the hillside green,

clean of human breath?

Studies of Rainwork

We are dulled into gray
    accents dripping from gutterless
thought and treeline, soaked from false
    impressions of sky.
We are dumbed into the minor
    drum, wet now with mistakes,
    mute with rain.

—

I am no stranger
    than the man metal-bent

under the accident of some
    fallen firmament.

I am soaked by an emergency
    of sunless sound. I am the man

umbrellaed by ambulance
    song, draining once more
his siren of color.

—

Our future is flooded with itself.
What is past dampens—
	just beyond a window
where the downpour locks us out.

The Parts of Clay Birds

When last we came,
we found parts of clay
birds, newspapers folded
into planes, an attic window
splintered, a novella stained
with old sun. At the far end, a makeshift
table served as a token of emptied
time, its legs four crates of unbound
books marked *this side up.* Our eyes
glanced wide, nodded, noted the cursive
description of a man set down
by another. Above, a fingerless
glove nailed to a joist
of light. One of us renounced
the noiselessness of our search.
We left him on the other side
of the room, where *The Book
of Ideal Wings* lay dark and singed.
Yes, some of us did stay on, clouding
the room with talk of shadows, and sight
did thin as evening clung just below
the eyes; for the whispery rush
of sleep reversed our steps, pinned

all things equal to the unfinished
walls on which the portraits of dead
hunters hung heavy, their eyes
like ours, gone to air and cracking.

Playing House

They sit together in the house
of always-going. He forgets

that his voice is a noise
inside walls. She stands

it. No, she is putting her hands
to her ears, her eyes to the walls.

She finds something in the wall, a thing
he cannot give her. They go on like this

in the house of always-going. He gets
up from his chair. He climbs the stairs

and comes back down. She is not
in the room he left her in. She is

in the kitchen slicing things up.
He remembers there is nothing

to say, and he goes about trying
to say this. She goes about the slicing.

He leaves her in the kitchen.
He climbs the stairs again.
There are kids here somewhere.

An Invitation to Speak

Or suppose I rose up, just
to fall nowhere in the hem
and haw of it, sighed the pock-
faced priest. Suppose I broke
with space, wounded time—so
wished the aging physicist
in the disquiet between things
and men. Or what can follow
hardly from them, cut in the lone
logician. Or suppose I defined
my difficulties, wheezed the ex-
philosopher, in dedication
to the sudden and severe
disappearance of principles
in children, dreamless and certain
of gnawing. Or suppose I turned dark
days into harsh light under
which no one can vanish, chimed
in the fat magician…a man-made
light…dimmed to make truth a trick
or treat in the clamoring act of give
then take, rolled the one false eye
of the two-faced prophet. And suppose
they all said what they said above…

a trapdoor. No doubt they would fall
for it, for the fear they were neither
here nor there, cried one of us,
blindfolded and moving along
the perimeter of his own voice.

Curse of the Self-sufficient

I read about arrowheads.
Lamplight from the sun-
room bends the mind

toward malady. I touch
the wound on my lower
lip, mouth the trajectory

of a single bloodless
thought. I could say
I was once the hunter
arriving at the nearest

conclusion. Or I could say
there is nothing to groan for—

but this alone.

The Idler Puts Himself at Risk

It is time, I say, to find
an ear in the ground,
to lay pith into it—
consolation of my own

echo. I say I must go,
be at large among
the growth, move

outside ambitions
beating me back.

—

Here comes the child-
cry I am wont to deny.

Here comes the child-
rhyme, my raw name

carved backward
in the bark and angle

of time. And against
my skin, the air feels
       a loss of sky.

—

Oh the bleating
lyricism of a goat
woos me—the cashmere
night too much to touch.

My face coins itself
an expression of oval
wind. I heap the instant

sadness on a scale
made from bird-bone
and my unused gravity.

The neck of my would-
be lover bends without

irony. There is much

classic and forked in
the myth of outside.

—

Look at me
says an ox

of a man, raving
by the riverside.

Look at me
I say into the river math.

Guesswork

What are we
to gain? Scraping
the last grammar
of love. The moon
broken to pieces

of luck. The rungless
ladder propped
against another
evening's guesswork.
Mark me: rope burns

inside the pale
gestures of flesh.
I never met a child

I was not. Could it be
this written above
the mountain? Could
it be a voice less

than mine sunk
into the blue fray?

Let me have

no new thing.

—

Acknowledgments

I offer my gratitude to the editors of the following publications in which some of these poems, or earlier versions, first appeared.

Asheville Poetry Review: "Of Shelter and Form"
The Boiler Journal: "Motion in a Path to Myself," "Undo
    Forces"
Mid-American Review: "The Metaphysician Goes Home"
Open Letters Monthly: "Determinism"
Tar River Poetry: "Playing House"
The Worcester Review: "Homecoming," "Verum
    and Factum"

Cover artwork, "Handy 4," by Billy Alexander; author photo by Claudia N. Theo; cover and interior book design by Diane Kistner; Congress with Arial Black titling

About FutureCycle Press

FutureCycle Press is dedicated to publishing lasting English-language poetry books, chapbooks, and anthologies in both print-on-demand and ebook formats. Founded in 2007 by long-time independent editor/publishers and partners Diane Kistner and Robert S. King, the press incorporated as a nonprofit in 2012. A number of our editors are distinguished poets and writers in their own right, and we have been actively involved in the small press movement going back to the early seventies.

The FutureCycle Poetry Book Prize and honorarium is awarded annually for the best full-length volume of poetry we publish in a calendar year. Introduced in 2013, our Good Works projects are anthologies devoted to issues of universal significance, with all proceeds donated to a related worthy cause. Our Selected Poems series highlights contemporary poets with a substantial body of work to their credit; with this series we strive to resurrect work that has had limited distribution and is now out of print.

We are dedicated to giving all of the authors we publish the care their work deserves, making our catalog of titles the most diverse and distinguished it can be, and paying forward any earnings to fund more great books.

We've learned a few things about independent publishing over the years. We've also evolved a unique, resilient publishing model that allows us to focus mainly on vetting and preserving for posterity the most books of exceptional quality without becoming overwhelmed with bookkeeping and mailing, fundraising activities, or taxing editorial and production "bubbles." To find out more about what we are doing, come see us at www.futurecycle.org.

The FutureCycle Poetry Book Prize

All full-length volumes of poetry published by FutureCycle Press in a given calendar year are considered for the annual FutureCycle Poetry Book Prize. This allows us to consider each submission on its own merits, outside of the context of a contest. Too, the judges see the finished book, which will have benefitted from the beautiful book design and strong editorial gloss we are famous for.

The book ranked the best in judging is announced as prize-winner in the subsequent year. There is no fixed monetary award; instead, the winning poet receives an honorarium of 20% of the total net royalties from all poetry books and chapbooks the press sold online in the year the winning book was published. The winner is also accorded the honor of being on the panel of judges for the next year's competition; all judges receive copies of all contending books to keep for their personal library.

www.ingramcontent.com/pod-product-compliance
Lightning Source LLC
LaVergne TN
LVHW020938090426
835512LV00020B/3422